To

_____

From

_____

Dear Dad

A Keepsake *of* Blessings *and* Memories
of Growing Up with You

Ellie Claire
gift & paper expressions

...inspired by life
EllieClaire.com

Ellie Claire® Gift & Paper Expressions
Brentwood, TN 37027
EllieClaire.com
Ellie Claire is a registered trademark of Worthy Media, Inc.

Dear Dad Journal
© 2014 by Ellie Claire
Published by Ellie Claire, an imprint of Worthy Publishing Group, a division of Worthy Media, Inc.

ISBN 978-1-60936-922-4

Stock or custom editions of Ellie Claire titles may be purchased in bulk for educational, business, ministry, fundraising, or sales promotional use. For information, please e-mail info@EllieClaire.com

Cover and interior design by Jeff and Lisa Franke | www.art-lab-studios.com

Printed in China

1 2 3 4 5 6 7 8 9 – 19 18 17 16 15 14

A father is neither
an anchor to hold us back,
nor a sail to take us there,
but a guiding light whose
love shows us the way.

Dear Dad,

This journal is just for us. It captures all my memories
and blessings of growing up with you. Some are funny,
some are heartwarming, some are bittersweet,
some are surprising, but all are reflections of my love for you.

There will be pages with full comments and some with
short comments and some with no comments.
But whether long or short, all the bits and pieces
have been personalized specifically to create
a one-of-a-kind keepsake just for you.

This gift comes from my heart. Thank you for all you have done,
are doing, and will do for me. I am blessed to call you Father.

Remember When...

There are cherished memories that I have tucked away to pull out and relive when I'm away or lonely or just need a "dad" moment—the "remember when?" times that brought us to tears either with laughter or sadness. The family get-togethers that we can never forget. The just-you-and-me moments that have made our relationship extra special. These are the shared memories I will always remember.

I thank my God every time I remember you.
In all my prayers for...you, I always pray with joy.
PHILIPPIANS 1:3 NIV

Remember when I wanted to be a...

*R*emember when you taught me to...

*R*emember when we laughed so hard about...

....

....

....

....

....

....

....

....

....

....

....

....

....

....

....

....

Remember when I would watch you while you...

*R*emember the family get-together when..

....

....

....

....

....

....

....

....

....

....

....

....

....

....

....

....

*R*emember when I got so mad because...

....

....

....

....

....

....

....

....

....

....

....

....

....

....

....

....

....

....

....

*R*emember when I tried to run away..

....

....

....

....

....

....

....

....

....

....

....

....

....

....

....

....

....

$\mathcal{R}$emember when we surprised...

*R*emember when we went on vacation and...

....

....

....

....

....

....

....

....

....

....

....

....

....

....

....

....

....

*R*emember when you told me about God...

$\mathcal{R}$emember when we had that conversation about……………………………………………………………

$\mathcal{R}$emember that movie I watched (or book I read) over and over.............................

....

....

....

....

....

....

....

....

....

....

....

....

....

....

....

....

....

Remember when I had my first date...

*R*emember when I first realized God could use me to...

....

....

....

....

....

....

....

....

....

....

....

....

....

....

....

....

....

....

....

....

....

....

My Favorite Things

As my dad, you know many of my favorite things. But there are some that may surprise you. This list includes a lot of my favorites, from the food that we ate to the birthday that is imprinted in my memory forever. Everything on this list pales in comparison to my very favorite thing on Earth—you!

We thank you, God, we thank you—your Name is our favorite word; your mighty works are all we talk about.

PSALM 75:1 MSG

My favorite memory of you is...

$\mathcal{M}$y favorite day spent outdoors with you was... ....
....
....
....
....
....
....
....
....
....
....
....
....
....
....
....
....
....
....
....
....
....
....

*M*y favorite project we worked on together...

....

....

....

....

....

....

....

....

....

....

....

....

....

....

....

....

....

....

*M*y favorite holiday tradition is..

....

....

....

....

....

....

....

....

....

....

....

....

....

....

....

....

....

*M*y favorite gift you ever gave me is...

$\mathcal{M}$y favorite family vacation was..

....

....

....

....

....

....

....

....

....

....

....

....

....

....

....

....

....

*M*y favorite room in our house growing up has to be...

....

....

....

....

....

....

....

....

....

....

....

....

....

....

....

....

....

....

....

*M*y favorite expression you use a lot is...

My favorite thing about you...

*M*y favorite birthday memory is... ....

....

....

....

....

....

....

....

....

....

....

....

....

....

....

....

....

....

....

....

....

....

....

*M*y favorite family pet is/was...

*M*y favorite place to hide was...

*M*y favorite song you sang or danced to was...

*M*y favorite book you read to me or encouraged me to read is...

We Are Stronger Because...

In every life there are things that are hard to get through. Thankfully for me, I had you as a dad to help guide me and make things right. You taught me lessons that made the hard things bearable and showed me, through love and by example, that hard things can be used by God to make us stronger. For that, I am extremely grateful.

We know that in all things God works for the good of those who love him, who have been called according to his purpose.

ROMANS 8:28 NIV

The hardest thing I ever had to tell you was...

$\mathscr{O}$ur family had to navigate a tough time when...

The time I saw you sacrifice for our family was...

The time I saw you give sacrificially for others was...

....

....

....

....

....

....

....

....

....

....

....

....

....

....

....

....

....

....

....

....

....

....

*T*he difficult time in our family when you demonstrated grace and/or mercy was...

....

....

....

....

....

....

....

....

....

....

....

....

....

....

....

....

....

....

*T*he thing that most frightened me and what you did to make it better was.............

....

....

....

....

....

....

....

....

....

....

....

....

....

....

....

....

....

....

....

I regret the time I made you feel..

*Y*ou helped me over that embarrassing moment by...

....

....

....

....

....

....

....

....

....

....

....

....

....

....

....

....

....

....

....

....

$\mathcal{T}$he punishment I remember most is...

The challenge I remember you struggling through for God was..

....

....

....

....

....

....

....

....

....

....

....

....

....

....

....

....

....

....

....

....

....

....

....

....

*Y*ou helped me overcome problems in school by..

....

....

....

....

....

....

....

....

....

....

....

....

....

....

....

*T*he thing about myself I don't like but you are helping me accept is… ....

....

....

....

....

....

....

....

....

....

....

....

....

....

....

....

....

....

....

....

The hardest thing about leaving home was..

The purpose I am seeing in my life because of you is...

....

....

....

....

....

....

....

....

....

....

....

....

....

....

....

....

....

....

....

....

NOTES, PHOTOS, CARDS

Lessons Learned

Even though I may not have expressed it often, I am thankful for all the lessons you've taught me. We haven't always agreed but I knew that you loved me and wanted the best for me. So you taught me lessons. Some I got right away. Some I am still learning. Thank you for continuing to teach me.

I applied my heart to what I observed
and learned a lesson from what I saw.

PROVERBS 24:32 NIV

The best lesson you ever taught me was... ....

....

....

....

....

....

....

....

....

....

....

....

....

....

....

....

....

The lesson about faith I most appreciate is...

The adage you repeated to me over and over that I wish I had listened to is..............

....

....

....

....

....

....

....

....

....

....

....

....

....

....

....

....

*T*he lesson that was hardest for me to learn is...

You taught me to respect others by..

....

....

....

....

....

....

....

....

....

....

....

....

....

....

....

....

The most important lesson you taught me about money was..

The nugget of wisdom I have cherished to this day is...

The lesson about the importance of family was demonstrated when..................................

....

....

....

....

....

....

....

....

....

....

....

....

....

....

....

....

You taught me to stand on my own two feet by...

*Y*ou taught me to accept my flaws by...

....

....

....

....

....

....

....

....

....

....

....

....

....

....

....

....

....

You taught me the importance of thinking before I act when...

....

....

....

....

....

....

....

....

....

....

....

....

....

....

....

....

....

....

....

....

....

The lesson I learned a little too publicly was...

....

....

....

....

....

....

....

....

....

....

....

....

....

....

....

....

The lesson I'm still trying to learn is...

The best advice you ever gave me was...

NOTES, PHOTOS, CARDS

Stories I Love

There are stories you have told that touch my heart;
stories that make me smile or roar with laughter.
Stories about grandparents and family and other people
who have come in and out of our lives. And there
are stories that I tell my friends about this wonderful
family we are part of. Here are a few of my favorites.

I will teach you hidden lessons from our past—
stories we have heard and known,
stories our ancestors handed down to us.

PSALM 78:2–3 NLT

My favorite story to tell is..

....

....

....

....

....

....

....

....

....

....

....

....

....

....

....

....

....

....

*T*he story I love about your kindness is...

The story I tell others when they ask about my dad is...

$\mathcal{M}$y favorite story that you told me is...

$\mathcal{T}$he story of an adventure that scared me silly but now makes me laugh is..................

....

....

....

....

....

....

....

....

....

....

....

....

....

....

....

....

....

....

$\mathcal{T}$he wild and crazy side of you is best seen in the story about...

....

....

....

....

....

....

....

....

....

....

....

....

....

....

....

....

....

My favorite story of you growing up is..

....

....

....

....

....

....

....

....

....

....

....

....

....

....

....

....

....

$\mathcal{M}$y favorite story you tell about me when I was little is..

....

....

....

....

....

....

....

....

....

....

....

....

....

....

....

The story about the best day of growing up with you for a dad is...

The accident story that I'll never forget is...

The story about our family get-together that still makes me chuckle is.................................

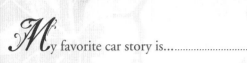

$\mathcal{M}$y favorite car story is...

....

....

....

....

....

....

....

....

....

....

....

....

....

....

....

....

....

The holiday story that I remember most is..

....

....

....

....

....

....

....

....

....

....

....

....

....

....

....

....

....

$\mathcal{M}$y favorite story told by a family member is...

....

....

....

....

....

....

....

....

....

....

....

....

....

....

....

....

....

....

....

NOTES, PHOTOS, CARDS

Relatives and Family Friends

Friends and family come in all shapes and sizes,
moods and dispositions, characters and personalities.
We've shared some great times, some hard times,
and some really memorable times with this cast of characters.
Thank you for allowing them to shape my life.

*Her neighbors and relatives heard that the Lord
had shown her great mercy, and they shared her joy.*

LUKE 1:58 NIV

The relative that makes me laugh the hardest is...

....

....

....

....

....

....

....

....

....

....

....

....

....

....

....

....

The most memorable family in our neighborhood was...

The friends that have always loved me like I'm family are...

....

....

....

....

....

....

....

....

....

....

....

....

....

....

....

....

The family road trip I remember most is..

....

....

....

....

....

....

....

....

....

....

....

....

....

....

....

....

....

....

The holiday that is best shared with the whole family is..

....

....

....

....

....

....

....

....

....

....

....

....

....

....

....

....

....

....

*T*he food we always have to eat at family get-togethers is..

....

....

....

....

....

....

....

....

....

....

....

....

....

....

....

....

....

The things I like best about your side of the family is...

....

....

....

....

....

....

....

....

....

....

....

....

....

....

....

....

$\mathcal{T}$he traits I inherited from our family that I love are...

....

....

....

....

....

....

....

....

....

....

....

....

....

....

....

....

....

....

....

....

....

....

*O*ur family is well-known for...

That thing about our family that makes me most proud is...

The friends that we shared life with while I was growing up were..

The funniest friend we had as a family was...

The family member who we most often tried to avoid was...

$\mathcal{T}$he friends or family members we most anticipated visiting were...............................

I Am So Thankful for You

More than anything, I am grateful to have you as my dad. We might not have been the perfect family, but we were perfect for each other. Thank you for just being Dad, for loving me unconditionally, for seeing in me things I could not see myself, for protecting me as I grew up in ways I cannot even now understand. From the bottom of my heart, I want to thank you for all you've done and all you've meant to me.

I give you thanks, O Lord, with all my heart.

PSALM 138:1 NLT

I am most grateful for your...

$\mathcal{I}$ am grateful and really proud of the way you helped our family by... ....

....

....

....

....

....

....

....

....

....

....

....

....

....

....

....

I am grateful for your ability to make me smile when you...

....

....

....

....

....

....

....

....

....

....

....

....

....

....

....

I am grateful for the relationships you modeled, like..

I am grateful for the prayers you've prayed for me and with me, especially..............

....

....

....

....

....

....

....

....

....

....

....

....

....

....

....

....

I am grateful for when you indulged me by...

I am grateful for the time you cheered me on by...

I am grateful for how you make me feel beautiful by...

....

....

....

....

....

....

....

....

....

....

....

....

....

....

....

....

....

I am grateful for when you stood up for what you knew was right by......................

....

....

....

....

....

....

....

....

....

....

....

....

....

....

....

....

....

I am grateful for how you influenced my personal faith by...

....

....

....

....

....

....

....

....

....

....

....

....

....

....

....

....

I am grateful for being alive after I...

I am grateful for the bandages and kisses when...

....

....

....

....

....

....

....

....

....

....

....

....

....

....

....

....

....

....

I am grateful that you let me try..

....

....

....

....

....

....

....

....

....

....

....

....

....

....

....

....

....

I am grateful that you were there for me when..

....

....

....

....

....

....

....

....

....

....

....

....

....

....

....

....

....

....

....

....

....

....

....

....

....

....

In My Own Words

There are some things that I just have to tell you—
things that are unique to our relationship. Or photos
that I want to show you with explanations or captions,
memories of my life with you. Or doodles I couldn't help
but draw of fun times or family trees that I think you'll enjoy.
In the next few pages, I want to let you know how much I love
and appreciate you...in my own words and in my own way.

These things we write to you that your joy may be full.

1 John 1:4 NKJV

God, being the God you are,
you have...blessed my family
so that it will continue
in your presence always.
Because you have blessed it,
God, it's *really* blessed—blessed for good!

1 Chronicles 17:26–27 MSG